CONTENTS

Title Page: Sweet Pickles Take Time	3
INTRODUCTION	5
DAY ONE	9
DAY TWO	14
DAY THREE	19
DAY FOUR	24
DAY FIVE	28
DAY SIX	32
DAY SEVEN	37
DAY EIGHT	41
DAY NINE	45
DAY TEN	49
DAY ELEVEN	55
DAY TWELVE	61

SWEET PICKLES
TAKE TIME

By Debra Yergen

This book is dedicated to my mom, sister and grandmas throughout history. To those who cook and those who love good food. May this nourish your body and soul.

INTRODUCTION

Welcome to twelve days of God's love and grandma's recipes. I come from a line of women who cook. No one ever left my parents house or my grandparents houses hungry. Even today, when mom and dad share stories of The Great Depression, there were two things folks could depend on: ample amounts of delicious food and grace before we ate.

There have always been so many wonderful recipes and food stories in our house. On the following pages, you'll find some of our favorite family recipes that have been passed down through the generations. It's my hope that these recipes will bring you as many special moments and memories as they have brought our family and a village of wonderful friends along the way.

It's hard to beat my Grandma Ursula's bread and butter pickles. Folks usually describe them merely as "perfect." They are a delightful combination of tangy and sweet.

A few years back, I realized that sweet pickles are a lot like prayer: they both take time. More on that ahead. When I delivered some bean soup to my uncle tonight, he told me how much he appreciated the warm hearty goodness, before asking, "You don't happen to have any of mom's sweet pickles left do you?" I laughed. It's winter and I have one jar left from last summer. Good thing his birthday is in March. I'm saving it for him.

Long before my mom was born, her parents owned a saloon called "Frank's Place." The saloon sat downtown below a floor of low-rent apartments. There was an old stubborn German, a violin maker, who barely spoke a word of English. He lived upstairs in the apartments after his wife Clara passed. He would get so engrossed in his craft that he'd often forget to eat. And sometimes when he finally realized he was hungry, instead of going out, he'd beat his violin bow on the pipes. And my sweet grandma, Ida Mae (who was affectionately called Susie by patrons and close friends alike) would ladle him up a hot bowl of chowder and tiptoe up the stairs with a spoon and extra napkins.

A few years after my parents were married, mom and dad were swapping stories one night and stumbled upon a amazing intersection of circumstances. Susie was my mom's mom and the violin maker was Julius Wolff, my dad's maternal grandfather. Grandma Ida Mae (Susie) shared her secret chowder ingredient with mom, and I've included it in this book.

One day at yoga, I made a new friend who rushed up to me after class when she heard my last name. Even before introducing herself, Kay excitedly blurted out, "How are you related to Grandma Yergen?"

"Which one?" I asked. Kay and her sister Maria had wonderful memories of Little Grandma, who although I never met, I knew by the marvelous stories from dad and his siblings about their dad's mom.

Kay gushed like a schoolgirl. "Stopping by Grandma Yergen's house after school for sugar cookies was among my sisters and my favorite childhood memories." Kay and I became fast friends with such a special lady in common.

I never met Grandma Olga. Dad and his siblings called her "Little Grandma" because she was small in stature and bent over with a hump on her back from scoliosis. Friends and family alike raved about Grandma Olga's sugar cookies; and once I made them, I had to agree. Even with gluten-free flour, those cookies are the bomb.

I've included some of my favorite family recipes from both my maternal and paternal grandmas on the following pages along with 12 days of devotionals intended to wrap you up in God's love.

There are two things I grew up trusting: God's love and grandmas' recipes. In good times and bad, these two things remain a consistent source of comfort to me. Hopefully, you will find comfort here as well.

DAY ONE

Are We There Yet?

I've met exactly one person my entire life who didn't like pickles. I've met some who love them more than others, and some who prefer bread-and-butter pickles over dills, or vice versa.

But most people enjoy some form of pickles, whether mixed into tuna salad, piled on hot dogs or hamburgers, diced into potato salad with mustard, mayo and eggs, sliced in sandwiches or just crunched deliciously right out of the jar.

I didn't realize how much my friends and family love pickles until I started canning them using my Grandma Ursula's recipe. Soon, my friends who had previously insisted on "no gifts" for birthdays and other special occasions started making exceptions, "Unless you have pickles, salsa, or orchard preserves."

This was music to my ears. Many of my friends were quite successful and had the means to purchase anything they desired. So what a compliment it was that of all the gifts in the world, they wanted my pickles and other canned goods. I loved that the items they wanted most were the ones I made with love in my kitchen. The ones I poured my time, talent and often ingredients from my own garden into.

This was all good and fine, until I noticed a problem. Many of my friends couldn't wait the six weeks necessary for the pickles to fully marinate. I would receive phone calls and text messages raving about Grandma Ursula's sweet pickles. And usually mid-message, there would be this pause, when they remembered I told them they had to wait six weeks.

The message would suddenly shift, with them assuring me that their jar of pickles had marinated more quickly than expected because the pickles were in a word – perfect!

I knew what I had to do. If my friends couldn't wait for the pickles, I would do the waiting for them. I started holding back the pickles until they were closer to pickle maturity.

Not long after one of my friends shared this news with me, of her pickles marinating early, I attended church one Sunday and the sermon hit home.

So many times I had prayed, even begged God, to send blessings or remove trials, petitioning my loving Savior to care for my needs in the way I hoped. And so many times I cried myself to sleep knowing He heard me, but feeling like He must not care enough about my struggle.

After hearing that sermon about waiting on God, I once again found myself in my kitchen canning, and His voice was so clear: *Sweet Pickles Take Time. And so do the lessons He leads us through.*

I can't count the number of times God has granted me a taste of His heavenly blessings at a difficult time in my life, when a mere taste left me craving more while it sufficiently reminded me of the feast awaiting. Other times, my life is brimming with blessing and I find myself exclaiming gratitude every few minutes. Gratitude for the sunrise or sunset gratitude that I experienced the majesty of an Eagle flying by, gratitude for a green light, or maybe a red light, preventing me from having an accident.

In all things, I have learned to express gratitude for what He has done, is doing or will do in my life.

Sweet Pickles Take Time is a powerful reminder that life does not unfold on our timetable. In fact, sometimes we find ourselves so far off our trail, and so far from the timetable, that we have no choice but to step back, find our compass and recalculate the path. But God is faithful and there is a purpose in even the most difficult of circumstances, weeks, months and years. The pickles will be ready someday and when they are ready, they will be worth the wait.

Today's Recipe:

Grandma Ursula's Bread and Butter Pickles (makes 6 quarts)

Ingredients:

8-10 pounds of pickling cucumbers (about 50-60, sized 3-5 inch cucumbers)
3/4 cup pickling salt
2 teaspoons alum, divided (found in spice isle or canning section of store)
4 cups ice
6 cups apple cider vinegar
8 cups granulated sugar
1 tablespoon celery seeds
3 tablespoons mustard seeds
12 cloves
4 bay leaves
4 teaspoons turmeric

Day One Directions:

1. Wash cucumbers and cut into 1/8 inch slices.
2. Place cucumber slices into a large bowl and toss with salt and 1 teaspoon alum. Gently toss to make sure salt and alum coat each slice. Cover with 4 cups of ice and cold water just to cover cucumbers. Top with a damp towel and let sit for at least 8 hours or overnight.

Day Two Directions:

1. Drain the cucumbers in a colander, rinse thoroughly with water, drain and repeat.
2. Sterilize jars, lids and rings in boiling water for 10 minutes. Remove to racks with tongs.
3. While jars are hot, pack each jar tightly with rinsed cucumber slices. Add an extra pinch of alum to each jar. If you have extra cucumber slices, create an extra "taster jar" by filling a clean, sterilized glass jar that will not be sealed but rather be refrigerated.
4. In a large pan, combine the apple cider vinegar, sugar, celery seeds, mustard seeds, cloves, bay leaves and turmeric. Bring to a boil. Reduce the heat to medium and simmer for 3 additional minutes.
5. Ladle the liquid spice mixture into the jars, running a knife down the insides of the jars to release any trapped air.
6. Gently screw on the lids. Process in a water bath for 25-30 minutes depending on your altitude. (If at high altitude, aim for 30 minutes.)
7. Let jars cool on racks until they naturally seal. Any that do not seal in 24 hours, put in the refrigerator with the extra "taster jar".

The pickles need to marinate in brine for 6 weeks. Yes, they may taste a bit like pickles in as little as 24 hours. Remembering that sweet pickles take time, you will find that the pickles you let sit for a solid six weeks will taste best. Refrigerate after opening. (If you want to test how your pickles are progressing, open your refrigerated taster jar about three weeks in and only eat 2 or 3 slices. Do this each week through weeks 6, 7 and 8, and experience what a difference a little more time can truly make.)

Store pickles for up to a year in a cool, dark place. (That's what Grandma Ursula's recipe says. My pickles never last a year!)

DAY TWO

Canning is like Prayer

Canning is like prayer. In the beginning, both can be terribly intimidating.

Many of us start out in both unsure of what to do or say. I remember as a kid growing up in Sunday School; I would cringe when the teacher would ask for volunteers t lead prayer.

In fact, I did everything to avoid getting called on to pray in front of the class at chapel. I would look down, get quiet, avoid eye contact, and even look like I was taking notes. I hated public speaking, especially when I was supposed to sound "appropriately churchy."

Unlike my classmate Becky, whose dad was a preacher, I was terrified of being singled out. Becky always knew what to say and she always sounded so appropriate. Not me. Praying was super stressful for me, even when I was alone, but especially combined with the pressure of having someone else hear and possibly critique me.

When my stalling tactics failed, and I did get called on, I remember feeling overcome by my nerves wrapping their way around my throat, choking my air so my voice came out a whisper. Each time it got easier. And *Doesn't God have a great sense of humor that I grew up to be a television news reporter and then later a spokesperson and public speaker?*

The good news is that both canning and praying get easier with practice and time.

Canning is actually easier than public praying for a child, it turns out. Today, I liken canning to the adult version of eighth grade science. When I'm feeling silly and mischievous, a crazy grin will slide across my face when I'm making preserves. I switch to an imaginary project where the fruit is actually dish soap, water, vinegar and food coloring and the pectin I'm adding is baking soda. Suddenly (in my imagination) the concoction erupts into a magnificent fountain of color, splashing all over the ceiling and I start squealing and turning around in circles. For the record, that has actually never happened. But it is a silly fantasy I've envisioned more than once.

So, stepping back into my adult world, that would never happen while canning preserves, providing you stick with the recipe and do not mix things like vinegar and baking soda.

When it comes to canning, you have your exact ingredients – that most of us learn to play around with after a while – the fruit and vegetables, sugar, vinegar and spices. Then you add specific elements: time and temperature. Then there are the random ingredients: pectin, citric acid and sometimes alcohol. The pH balance has to be correct (which it is, when you use a proven recipe). Proper sterilization is non-negotiable (if you want to live and not get sick), and processing steps need to be followed according to your altitude.

It sounds complicated. But it's not.

For a lot of people prayer feels complicated, and it can feel intimidating, especially in front of other people. But it's really no different than a conversation.

Before Jesus performed his first miracle in John 2 of turning water into wine at the wedding of Cana in Galilee, the whole event started with a conversation. Can you imagine what that must have been like?

My mentor was a Jewish lady in Mercer Island, Washington, and I've had many close Jewish friends over the years, so I have some solid experience with traditional Jewish mothers. The ones I have known have held very high standards for excellence and hospitality. They've all been gracious perfectionists who how to throw a gala, and they never ran out of food or wine. I can't imagine Jesus' mother being any different. In true Jewish mother fashion, when she saw the wedding party had run out of wine, she jumped in to fix the situation. Isn't that fabulous?

Jesus hesitated initially. He wasn't sure His time had come to start performing miracles, but Mary believed in Him. She told the household staff to do whatever Jesus said, and they clearly took her seriously, immediately gathering six stone water pots. It's such a fun story, and one I always enjoy reading. As you read it, you can almost envision the urgency of this festive atmosphere.

Of course the outcome was great! The best part is when the governor of the wedding tastes the wine and is absolutely appalled at the bridegroom for saving the very best wine to the end of party. "Every man at the beginning doth set forth good wine; and when men have well drunk, then that which is worse: but thou hast kept the good wine until now."

Often times in cooking, it's acceptable to use a cooking or table quality wine. But canning is a different story. In canning, the fruit picks up the flavor of the alcohol. So if you want good results, you need to start with a quality preservative.

In the Yakima Valley, where I grew up, one of the first major harvests to ripen in June and July are is cherries. If you want to spoil your friends and family at Christmas, can up a dozen jars of Candies Brandy Cherries. This is a super easy recipe to make when you're learning to can. There are only three ingredients: tree-ripened cherries, brandy and sugar, outside of a bit of water.

I've seen this recipe with cinnamon, cloves and nutmeg but if you use a high-quality brandy or cognac, you don't need all those other spices. They just complicate flavors and detract from your brandy. Try it different ways if you like but this was my grandma's recipe.

◆ ◆ ◆

Today's Recipe:

Candied Brandy Cherries (makes 12 half-pints)

Ingredients:

4 pounds tree-ripened sweet Bing cherries, stemmed and pitted
2 cups Korbel brandy (or a high quality brandy of your choice)
2 cups sugar
1/2 cup water

Directions:

1. Sterilize jars, lids and rings.
2. Wash, stem and pit cherries.
3. Tightly pack cherries into sterilized jars. How much liquid you need will depend partly on how tightly you pack your cherries. If you run low on syrup, it's easy to mix up more. The formula is always equal parts brandy and sugar and half as much water. Some people like to cook their cherries in the syrup but then they don't have the same beautiful form when you open the jar and gently cascade them over ice cream or another favorite dessert. I hand pick each cherry in the orchard for my candied brandy cherries so I pack snug but not tight, and I do not cook them in the syrup.
4. Mix together water and sugar - always half as much water as sugar. So 1 cup sugar to 1/2 cup water. Bring this to a boil. You

want your sugar fully dissolved. Remove from heat source and stir in the same amount of brandy (1 cup) as sugar.

5. Pour beautiful rich liquid over cherries, leaving 1/4 inch headspace at the top of the jar. Wipe the jar rim with a damp paper towel. Add lid and ring. Finish with all 12 little jars, making more brandy syrup if necessary with the same ratio.

6. Transfer jars to a pan filled with water, making sure the water is at least 2 inches deeper than the top of your jars. The great thing about making half pint jars is that most people have pans that are deep enough without purchasing larger canning pans required to water bath quart jars. So this is a great recipe to use when you're learning to can or new to canning.

7. Boil or process jars for 25 minutes. Remove to towel on counter or rack to cool.

Any jars that do not seal in 24 hours should be refrigerated. With such a high alcohol content and sugar, the fruit will last longer than preserves. The other reason I do not cook my cherries in the syrup is because I know they will naturally cook in the water bath and I prefer to keep them as firm to be enjoyed six months later.

DAY THREE

Breaking It Down

Prayer can begin like any other conversation, with a salutation or greeting. How do we greet a friend or someone we're happy to see? A conversation with God also starts with hello. And just like pickles begin with a recipe, Jesus taught us how to pray using the example of *The Lords' Prayer in Matthew 6*.

"It's amazing to see you. You look fantastic!" is a great way to be greeted by someone important to us. We love to be greeted with a happy tone or a compliment.

Of course God loves it when we greet Him with joy, praise and acknowledgement for all He has done and will do in our circumstances and lives. As humans, those of us who believe in a Creator with a grand design, also understand that as part of the created universe, we're part of a larger plan. So we surrender to the Creator as we request help, guidance and provision in our lives, acknowledging our own shortcomings and in turn forgiving other people for their shortcomings.

We all need help in some way along our journey – help for those concerns we bring to the Lord and protection from the forces around us and within us. Isn't it amazing to know that as bad as our struggles can be, we are not alone in facing them? That's certainly worthy of our thanksgiving and praise. We know from *Romans 8:28, All things work together for the glory of God.*

There are people who need help. They need our prayers, and they need to know that someone sincerely cares for them. Sometimes, we're the ones who need help. What if the whole purpose for "struggle" in life is to teach us to help those who we can help and give those around us the opportunity to help us?

Sometimes, the boldest, most confident, outspoken people on the outside, are the ones who struggle the most with finding the courage to ask for help or prayer. How are we even to know that someone with so much confidence really needs our support or prayer?

When we listen carefully, we hear others asking for help. Sometimes, their requests come indirectly. Sometimes their petitions come as whispered suggestions that are easy to miss. Sometimes they make a comment or hesitate when asked a question. Maybe we notice that the emotion in their eyes doesn't match their words. If we're open to supporting them with prayer, the Holy Spirit helps us see and hear their cries for help in places we may have otherwise missed.

I am connected on social media to one of the noisiest, self-congratulating, mega-confident women I've ever met. We met through a shared association and up until a fateful Thirsty Thursday several months back, I did my best to avoid her public tirades about how enormously successful she is. Then one Thursday afternoon, I was meeting a girlfriend for happy hour and when I stepped into the restaurant bar, there she was: the woman I silently avoided by all means possible.

I pretended like I didn't see her, and then she called out my name and motioned me over to the empty bar stool beside her. I cringed on the inside but smiled on the outside and walked over to where she was sitting.

Unexpectedly, she proceeded to open up and share her heart about her worries, fears and flaws. One-on-one she was nothing like the image she posted online. In person, she was vulnerable, humble and scared. And then it happened. She asked me to pray for her, right there in a bar.

I never dreamed someone who boasted such great success would ever even hint, let alone ask, for me to actually care and pray for her. But she did. She dropped the veil, and I was faced with a choice. I had been asked to step up in love.

Maybe someone in your greater circle of friends and acquaintances made a comment on social media. Or perhaps a name or situation jumped out at you from the bulletin at church. Perhaps you're seated next to someone on a train or at a doctor's office who unexpectedly shared their heart, story or emotions in a way that indicated they need support. These are all ways the Holy Spirit prompts us to pray for others.

We live in a broken, hurting world. We are surrounded by people who need God's love, grace and provision as much as we do.

I can only imagine my grandma explaining, *dear child, the field is ripe with cucumbers, ready to be harvested and turned into delicious sweet pickles.*

Maybe, more than a half century later, I could learn from Susie. She offered her hands to share God's provision with her future daughter's future husband's poor hungry great grandfather, Julius, kindly offering an old man a cup of warm chowder and extra napkins.

Today's Recipe:

Susie's Pub Chowder (makes 2 quarts)

Ingredients:

1/2 pound bacon
1 large sweet onion, chopped fine
4 cups potatoes, peeled and cubed (small cubes)
2 cups water
2 cups milk
2 cups whipping cream
2 tablespoons flour (or cornstarch dissolved in cold water if you're glutenfree)
1 1/2 teaspoons salt
1 teaspoon Old Bay seasoning
1/4 cup butter
2 pounds cleaned razor clams or butter clams, diced small (or two 10oz cans of clams in clam juice)
1 cup clam juice
Ground black pepper to taste

Directions:

1. Chop raw bacon and sauté over medium heat in large stockpot. Cook until crisp and add finely diced onions. Cook 5 additional minutes.
2. Stir in water and potatoes. Season with salt, pepper and Old Bay. (Old Bay was grandma's secret ingredient. Mom loves Old Bay too and some years, for Christmas, sister and I find a can wrapped up in our stockings.)
3. Add butter, clams and clam juice. Add 8oz jar if canned clams were used or just use the juice from the clams if fresh clams were used + extra clam juice if necessary to equal 1 cup. A little extra clam juice won't hurt. It just gives you more chowder. Bring to boil and simmer on medium until potatoes are cooked through

(about 25 minutes).
4. Test to make sure the potatoes and clams are tender. Simmer on medium until they are tender.
5. Bring soup back to a boil and add flour. (If you opt for a glutenfree version, dissolve cornstarch in a half cup of cold water and pour into boiling chowder. Stir until the cloudiness resolves. The glutenfree adaptation was not in grandma's recipe. I added it because I'm celiac and it's how I make her chowder today.)
5. Once the chowder is at the thickness you prefer, bring the temperature down to a light simmer and add the milk and whipping cream.

Serve hot but do not boil the milk-based ingredients.

DAY FOUR

Blessings Make Life More Enjoyable

Some people love to hear how cute their shoes are. I love that too, but I love it more when my friends and family rave about my homemade pickles or something I've poured a part of myself or talents into. It's not that I need to hear praise for a job well-done. I follow a recipe so I know my pickles are going to turn out consistently delicious. Hearing my friend rave reminds me that something simple I made with my hands and heart brings joy to the people in my life.

When someone tells me how much they enjoyed the flavor of one of my baked, cooked or canned treats, I receive the gift of knowing that something small I made gave someone else joy. One of my water-walking friends once enjoyed an entire jar of my strawberry rhubarb jam in one sitting while watching TV. To be fair, it was a small jar. She's told that story at the pool a dozen times, always with this expression of pure joy on her face. And her expression makes me feel wonderful every single time.

What a blessing to me it is that my sweet pickles, salsa, preserves and candy brandy cherries are repeatedly transformed into blessings for my friends and family; their gratitude is the blessing back to me. The same is true with prayer.

Prayer is the single most important gift we can offer on behalf of each other. Unfortunately, the phrase "thoughts and prayers" can be used almost as a trite catchphrase by some people. This can make the expression less meaningful to some, but it in no way diminishes the power of prayer. Instead of imagining the intentions or the sincerity of another person, I accept this phrase as a gift. Sometimes it's a genuine gift by someone who is praying for me or others who are in need or hurting. Sometimes it is what that person wishes they could give or feels it is what they ought to say. I call this a seed.

Imagine grandma's words of wisdom: *We don't get to watch every seed grow. But every seed that's planted has a better chance of growing than one that isn't.*

To me, prayer is like bacon. It makes everything better. Prayer changes circumstances. It heals, comforts and wraps others and us in an invisible shield of peace and grace.

Have you ever found yourself in a stressful situation and suddenly you were overcome by a sense of peace and serenity? It's probably because someone was praying for you in that moment.

God loves to grant us blessings and it makes Him so happy when we say thank you. Which begs the questions: *Why does He often make us wait through the trials? Why does He say no when we ask for healing or help? Why do children and loved ones die or suffer seemingly senselessly?*

Why do hearts break and relationships fracture? Why do natural disasters happen and why do some people seem to slide by while others endure years of struggle and trauma?

Growing up, my sister and I loved salads from the time we were very young. Growing up on an apple farm, mom almost always cooked homemade meals, and always in the same proportion: a protein (meat), a vegetable (usually something hot) and a salad.

This was the early 1980s so it was before awareness of The Zone Diet, Mediterranean Diet or anything else suggesting how many servings of fruits and vegetables a day were widely considered.

One of our favorite salads came from our mom's mom. Mom didn't serve this velvety delight very often, but every time she did, it was received with squeals and joy. Probably, because everything's better with bacon!

Today's Recipe:

Grandma's Tangy Wilted Bacon Salad

Salad ingredients:

4 cups romaine lettuce, torn
1/2 pound bacon

Dressing ingredients:

2 tablespoons of bacon grease
1 egg
1/2 cup vinegar
1/2 cup sugar

Directions:

1. Wash and tear romaine into bite-size pieces. Arrange on a platter or individual salad plates.
2. Fry bacon to the point where it is crispy. Drain on paper towels.
3. Crumple bacon across the top of the prepared romaine.
4. Once the romaine and bacon crumbles are in place, it's time to make the dressing.
5. Discard bacon grease except for 2 tablespoons of bacon grease. Beat 1 egg with a fork. Add vinegar and sugar and beat again. Turn on heat source and reheat bacon grease on medium. Slowly add the egg/vinegar/sugar mixture, stirring continuously with a fork. You just want to heat this mixture until the egg is warmed and

partially cooked all the way through. The very warm dressing should still be light enough to drizzle over the romaine.

6. Immediately pour the velvety dressing lightly over the top of the plated salad, wilting the romaine, and serve.

DAY FIVE

Can God Really Do Anything?

A confession is in order here: It's hard for me to wait too. Even though I know the pickles will turn out, and I trust the process, I do more than keep a "taster" jar in my refrigerator with a pickling date so I can check how the pickles are coming along each week. Sometimes, I open the taster jar in between "taste tests" because I'm craving a sweet pickle.

God holds all of life's great recipes in His hand. So it reasons that He can do anything. *So if He can do anything, in an instant, why does our loving and merciful God sometimes go crickets or radio silent on us? And why, when He sees yesterday, today and tomorrow does He allow things like disease and unspeakable violence to ever occur? Why doesn't He step in and stop them?* These questions, as they relate to specific circumstances, are such that only God knows the answers.

In a greater context, God can only be true to His word. Part of His design was to give humans freewill. And sometimes the freewill of one person causes great pain to another.

When I was in high school, a teacher crossed a line by pulling me into his office away from the other students and touching me inappropriately. Having him pet and fondle me and telling me he loved me and I was a special student to him was a clear violation of trust. His words were nice but his actions were very uncomfortable and confusing.

After the second time it happened, I visited the principal's office to seek help; the principal immediately pulled me out of that teacher's class and reassigned me to another class. Neither the teacher nor the principal ever apologized, and it left me feeling like adults and specifically men failed to protect me. Years later, in a SOZO prayer, designed to trace fears and challenges in my adult life back to events in my childhood, I wondered where Jesus Christ was in the middle of this traumatic childhood experience.

As I relived the experience, I saw Christ across the room and He beckoned me to him. When I walked to Christ in my vision, He reached out and comforted me, providing the safety I never felt in that teacher's office before. For me, the fear and the pain of that childhood trauma melted away. I even forgave the teacher. When I asked the SOZO prayer guides why Christ failed to protect me when I was a kid, they said that He was always there, but to take away the teacher's freewill to harm his student, would have gone against God's greater promise and design to create humankind in His own image, with freewill and the ability to decide right from wrong.

What we know, according to *Jeremiah 29* is that *God knows the plans He has for us and that His plans are ultimately to prosper us and not to harm us.* This message was originally written to the surviving Jewish elders, priests and other tribe people by the Prophet Jeremiah after they had been led into exile by Nebuchadnezzar, from Jerusalem to Babylon. No doubt they were tired and defeated, watching their neighbors and family members suffer and die in exile.

How exciting is it that the God of the Universe saw their pain and sent a message through His prophet Jeremiah to give comfort and encouragement at such a difficult time?

Have we not all felt this way at one time or another? Have we not all wondered how much more we can endure, or how much our family, friends, community or nation can endure? It's difficult and sometimes painful to wait upon the Lord when we need, want and pray for healing. In the middle of trials, it's challenging to accept that we are collectively part of a much greater plan for humanity.

God understands this. He doesn't ask us to wait to cause us more pain, but rather because He is working all things for our good, both the good in our lives and the good of drawing us near to Him. He's turning cucumbers into sweet pickles. We have to trust the process.

One of my favorite childhood sandwiches was actually a recipe from my mother's dad. He died before I was born and there aren't a lot of fluffy, yummy stories about him. My assessment of him, based on stories from mom and her brother, was that he enjoyed being stubborn, rigid and grumpy.

Born in 1900, he was nearly a half a century old when my mom came along, and more than a century old when her brothers, Rick and Robert, were born. He lived through the Roaring 20s and The Great Depression. In those days, it was Frank's way or the highway. I don't how we would have gotten along.

I do love his strange little sandwich that in 2018, *Food 52* named "Best of the Weird Sandwiches." It was created using the strangest combination of kitchen staples. It sounds terrible, but as mom instructed sister and me the first time she made it for us, "Don't knock it until you try it."

So despite his disposition, he left humanity something quite delicious. In fact, I think I might just make one now.

Today's Recipe:

<u>Grandpa Barth's 'Best of the Weird' Sandwich</u>

Ingredients:

2 slices of bread
2 teaspoons mayonnaise
1 tablespoon peanut butter
1 large leaf of iceberg lettuce
3 slices dill pickle

Directions:

1. Smooth the mayonnaise on 1 slice of bread and the peanut butter on the other slice.
2. On the slice with mayonnaise, line up the slices of dill pickle.
3. On the slice with the peanut butter, add the leaf of iceberg lettuce.
4. Put the sandwich together with the pickles and lettuce touching, slice and enjoy.

NOTE: In talking to my 95-year-old cousin, Isabelle, who was a first cousin to Grandpa Frank, I learned he gleaned this recipe from his mom, Great Grandma Eva.

"Honey, we were poor. We ate peanut butter on everything. Peanut butter was a good protein source and it didn't spoil during the day in a sandwich like meat did," Isabelle explained.

Isabelle had some other great family recipes I'll share and some charming stories about growing up nearly a century ago.

DAY SIX

Cutting Away The Imperfections

There's a secret farmers know when it comes to fruit. The flawed fruit is the sweetest. When I was a kid, mom used to have sister and me gather the injured apples, peaches and pears. Whether the skin had been pierced by something knocking into it or a bird peck, or a summer hail storm beat down on it, we always picked up the culls.

To help defray the cost of harvest, our family sold apples from our house, for only three dollars a box, and later ten cents a pound, to customers who came back year after year for dad's delicious apples.

One day I asked mom why our family always used the injured fruit for pies and salads and saved the perfect-looking fruit for customers. "Because they don't know the secret," she whispered, pulling me close and cradling my head.

"What secret?" I asked. Mom explained that when a piece of fruit or limb is injured during the growing season, the tree sends sap and sugar to the injured area. The apples that had been poked or suffered damage were actually sweeter than the perfect ones right beside them on the same tree.

Of course I insisted on a side-by-side taste test to verify this, and sure enough, the injured apples were sweeter. Once the imperfections were trimmed away, our family enjoyed the sweetest fruit from the orchard.

There have been many times in my life where my prayers consisted of three simple words: *Please help me.* Many nights I have fought through the tears, repeating just those three words. When I am unable to articulate my concerns, I trust the Holy Spirit to represent my needs on my behalf.

There have been times in life when I was too broken, defeated or discouraged to utter anything beyond a brief plea for help, and I know I am not alone in that. Life can be so very hard at times.

Maybe you have been there too, or known someone who has. Maybe you are there right now.

Instead of being discouraged by current circumstances, we can rejoice, understanding that petitions of lament and frustration lifted up are actually prayers of hope for the redemption that is coming. Even when you believe just a little that your prayers will be answered, you are practicing hope that good will prevail over pain, in this life or the next.

The beautiful thing is that our all-knowing God, Creator of the Universe, already knows everything about us. He sees us and loves us in this broken state, and He promises to provide. *Luke 12:24 says, Consider the ravens: They do not sow nor reap, they have no storeroom or barn; yet God feeds them. And how much more valuable are you than any birds!*

Of course He knows the pressures and concerns on our hearts. But He still wants to hear about them from us. He longs to have fellowship with His creation. Isn't it incredible that the God of the universe invites us to boldly speak our requests and the concerns of our hearts to Him?

We can trust the mystery of prayer knowing God loves every single person, and He is fully at work on our behalf.

In the beginning, God visited in the flesh with Adam in the Garden of Eden. *He walked with him and talked with him*, we learn in *Genesis 3:8*. And He walks and talks with us today through the Holy Spirit.

God wants fellowship with us. *I Corinthians 1:9 reminds us that God is faithful always.*

When we have family and friends with whom we wish to build a relationship, we share our time, talents, conversation and hearts. We listen and we trust them with the things that matter to us. The same is true about God.

Sometimes when I am canning pickles or even sweet, pretty peaches, I have to cut away a part of the fruit or vegetable that will be used in the final product. I don't want the rot or bitterness to taint the flavor of my final prepared jar. I smile always as I remember mom's demonstration when I was a child.

I don't throw out the entire cucumber, tomato or peach because it has a flaw I need to remove. I'm selectively choosing the sweetest, crispest, very best part of the ingredients to be included in that prized jar that will ultimately bring someone special a great deal of joy and fulfillment.

Through the challenges of life, God refines us, cutting away our imperfections and drawing us closer to Him. He loves us enough to transform our harvest into the sweetest batches, knowing the process will require trust and time.

Today's Recipe:

Grandma Ida Mae's Pretty Peaches

I actually learned to can peaches from my sister. But her recipe came from mom, and mom's recipe came from her mom. Another winning grandma recipe!

Ingredients:

Fresh peaches (about 3 pounds of fresh ripe fruit per canned quart)
3 cups sugar
1 tablespoon lemon juice
6 cups of boiling water
6 cups of ice water
4 cups water, filtered or distilled

Directions:

1. Prepare your jars, lids and rings by cleaning them well and adding them to water to bring to a boil. My preference is to add a cool or warm jar to cold water and bring both to a boiling point together. When canning, it's critically important that anything that touches food be properly sterilized. This easy but critical step prevents an environment where bacteria can enter, grow and potentially make someone sick.
2. Create your syrup mixture. Sugar is a preservative in canning. Your sugar-to-water ratio will depend on how heavy you like your syrup. Grandma's recipe called for 3 cups of sugar dissolved in 4 cups of water.
3. In a saucepan mix 3 cups of sugar in 4 cups of filtered or distilled water and bring to a boil to dissolve the sugar. Set aside.
NOTE: If you like a very heavy syrup, mix equal parts sugar and water: 4 cups of sugar to 4 cups of water. I prefer a light syrup so I usually mix 2 cups sugar to 4 cups of water. You can also select whatever you prefer between the two.
4. Prepare your fruit. In 6 cups boiling water, add a few peaches at a time for 30 seconds.
5. Remove them to 6 cups of ice water.
6. Slide the skins off the blanched peaches. Slice them into a bowl and sprinkle lemon juice over the top. Once your peaches are peeled, raw pack them into your sterilized jars.
7. Add one pit per jar. This keeps the fruit firm and adds flavor. Or maybe good luck. Grandma always added a pit, and since this is

her recipe, I add a pit in every jar.

NOTE: Raw packing just means you slice the fruit, turn it a few times in the bowl with lemon juice (to keep your fruit looking bright and fresh) and then place your slices in the jar. I like to pack my fruit pretty tightly so I don't end up with "floating fruit" after I add the hot syrup.

8. Bring your syrup back to a boil and pour it gently over your sliced peaches, leaving 1/2 to 1/4 inch head space at the top. Take a case knife and slide it down the insides of your jar. You will probably see tiny bubbles rise to the surface. This helps the air escape to eliminate the "floating fruit" later.

9. Wipe the rim of the jar with a clean damp paper towel. Add the lid and ring.

10. Finish filling your jars with fruit and syrup. Add them to a large pot for a water bath. You will need a minimum of 2 inches of water above the top of your closed jar. Process pints for 25 minutes or quarts for 40 minutes in boiling water. This is called water bath processing. If you live on a mountain or other high altitude, add five minutes.

11. Once the jars have finished processing, use tongs to move the jars from the boiling water to a towel on a nearby counter. Allow them to come to room temperature. As the jars cool, the lids will seal and you will possibly hear a small pop with each one.

12. If jars do not seal within 24 hours, refrigerate them and use them right away. In all of my years of canning peaches, I've only had 1 jar that did not seal, and that was my fault because I accidentally had 2 lids on 1 jar under the ring.

DAY SEVEN

Investing the Time

Waiting can be unbearably hard. It can feel unnecessary and even unfair.

Have you ever been in the middle of a large project that felt overwhelming, as if it would never end? Even if you intellectually knew it would end, were there moments you felt like it might never end? This is normal when we are waiting and growing.

Sometimes we are growing a *Fruit of the Spirit*, like patience. We are all familiar with praying to have patience, NOW! (So many jokes about that!) *According to Galatians 5, the Fruits of the Holy Spirit include love, joy, peace, patience, kindness, goodness, faithfulness, gentleness and self-control.* For those who practice Catholicism, they get to add five more: *charity, generosity, faith, modesty and chastity.* Can you guess what all of these have in common? Yes, time. The Fruits of the Spirit require time. None of them happen magically or instantly overnight.

So here we are, as humans, in the middle of this trial (whatever that may be in your life right now) and we're asking for relief, and we're wondering: *Dear Lord, why haven't you answered my prayer?*

The waiting can make us feel like we are losing our minds (and questioning our faith) sometimes. In these moments, the only way to stop obsessing about what we need and want is to make good use of our time.

Making good use of our time can take many forms. It may be simply setting aside our concerns to focus on other projects. When I was job hunting, I sent out more than 300 resumes. It was so discouraging. I would remind God: *You promised You would provide. I know you hear me. I know you see my tears and feel my worry.* But beyond doing what I needed to do, I had to find a way to make good use of my time.

I cleaned out my closets as I prepared for a possible move. I polished up my Christmas card list. It wasn't easy. In fact it was discouraging and painful.

Sometimes, waiting isn't so much about getting to tomorrow as it is about getting through today. In these situations, volunteering to help a local organization or church might calm the mind through busy hands.

While prayer is always powerful, and always heard, when our prayers become a repetitive loop (please help, please heal, please change a heart), sometimes it's healthier to find a meaningful way to sidetrack our thoughts by refocusing on something or someone else. When the Bible says to *pray without ceasing* in *1 Thessalonians 5:17*, it is derived from the Greek word "adialeiptos" is doesn't mean to pray without ever stopping, but rather to pray in a way that is constantly recurring.

God wants us to continue to bring our concerns to Him in a healthy way that doesn't drive us crazy or induce anxiety.

Once that jar of cucumbers is mixed with all the right spices and vinegar, sealed, water-bathed and set on racks, the only element left to turn them into pickles is time.

Waiting is hard and sometimes painful. It may include surviving a long winter that seems to never end, tirelessly job hunting through unemployment, staying positive through the weeks and months of undergoing an invasive treatment like chemotherapy (for yourself or a dear one), serving as a short-term or long-term caregiver, helping your children get through their teenage years, or any other difficult period of waiting. Waiting can wipe us out physically, mentally and emotionally.

I have heard from family and friends that my dad's Little Grandma Olga had a wonderful remedy for getting through life's most trying times.

She made sugar cookies. These were not just any sugar cookies.

These had a special secret ingredient: buttermilk. Buttermilk is basically sour milk that doesn't taste so hot to drink from a glass but cooks up to add the perfect flavor to cookies, breads and other homemade goodness. In fact, if you don't have buttermilk for a recipe, you can add lemon juice to milk and come up with something very close to use in baked recipes.

Today's Recipe:

Grandma Olga's Sugar Cookies (makes 2 dozen)

Ingredients:

3 cups all-purpose flour (I use gluten-free baking flour)
1 1/2 teaspoons baking powder
1/2 teaspoon salt
1 cup sugar
1 cup butter (2 cubes)
1 egg, beaten
3 tablespoons buttermilk
1 teaspoon vanilla extract

Directions:

1. Heat oven to 400 degrees F.
2. Combine the dry ingredients. Crosscut both cubes of cold butter into 200 tiny pieces drop them into the dry ingredients. Cut and blend with a pastry blender until the mix looks like tiny crumbles.
3. In a separate bowl, beat 1 egg, add buttermilk and vanilla and then whip together with a fork.
4. Pour the wet ingredients into the dry ingredients mixed with butter. Continue to combine and use your hands to form a ball. Roll dough out to 1/8". Generously sprinkle with sugar. Use the ring of a small mouth canning jar to cut circles.
5. Transfer raw cookie dough rounds to a non-greased metal pan. Bake 7-9 minutes.
6. Let cool on a cookie rack and serve.
(Frosting optional.)

DAY EIGHT

Pushing Through Disbelief

There is this strange joy that comes with the unexpected pop of a canned jar sealing. Every canning recipe explains that jars that do not seal within 24 hours of a water bath need to be refrigerated. But 24 hours can be a long time to wait when you want to know that all your jars sealed.

The first several years of canning, I would anxiously await hearing my jars seal. I would check on them, sometimes feeling temped to push down the seal but knowing I should not.

A perfectly sealed jar does not need, require or benefit from a human rushing the process. The process is what it is. Sometimes, in a batch of jars, only half of them would seal before I went to bed. I had to wait on the other half until morning. It would be exciting to get up for water overnight and hear a pop in the darkness, alerting me that another jar sealed.

An experienced canner is increasingly less tempted by the sealed jars sitting on the counter racks. He or she foregoes any inclination to open the sealed jars early, knowing whatever is inside will be perfect when the right time comes to open the jar. When we beg God to answer our prayers before it's time, He is not temped to grant our requests. To us it can feel as if he doesn't understand the urgency of our need.

In Mark 5, Jesus was talking to a large crowd of people when one of the synagogue leaders, named Jairus, saw Jesus and fell at his feet. He begged Jesus to come quickly and heal his daughter who was dying. Jesus followed Jairus, but He took His sweet time.

He stopped to talk to the crowd and interact with a woman who was healed by touching His garment. And just as Jairus was undoubtedly worried that they might not arrive in time, a person delivered the news he feared most: "Your daughter is dead. Why bother the teacher (Jesus) anymore?"

But the message Jesus shared with Jairus in this moment is the same message He shares with us: "Don't be afraid. Just believe."

Imagine knowing your child died but having the Savior tell you to set fear aside and just believe. In a short time, Jesus took the hand of this 12-year-old girl and said to her, "*Talitha koum!*" which means, "*Little girl, I say to you, get up.*" And she immediately did.

God can reverse our most devastating fears and heal our greatest pain. This seldom happens on our timetable.

We have all had doors shut that we prayed would be opened. Some people believe that one day we will have all our questions answered and we will understand. It could be that. It also could be that someday, when we are united with Christ Jesus in heaven, all the things that troubled us on Earth will no longer matter compared to the glory that awaits.

God knows the plans He has for us, the plans for our best possible outcome, and He wants for us to enjoy the very best of His gifts – either in this life or the life to come.

My mom tells a story of her genuine disbelief as a new bride when my dad shared with her their Yergen Family Christmas tradition of serving fried oysters on Christmas Eve. This was all new to her. But she was young and eager to please her new husband and his family, so she went along with it.

Sweet Pickles Take Time

It might be like marrying into a family that grew up eating pinecones or squirrels. Nonetheless, she powered through like a trooper. She may have just started learning her way around a kitchen, but her meal was perfect, and no one else was surprised her fried oysters were a hit!

Over the past 50 years, mom has hosted dozens of family members, family members of family members, friends and friends of family. Most people start by taking one oyster on their plate to be polite, but return for seconds and thirds, often year after year. It's one more example of how pushing through disbelief can result in abundant joy.

Sometimes, on the journey to create the most delicious jar of sweet pickles, God cuts away some of the things we want most. This would be unbearable, if it weren't for the fact that He delivers other blessings we never imagined, in place of the doors He allows to shut.

It's only after we open that fully-brined and ready-to-eat jar of sweet pickles, that we understand or accept that His recipe was in our best interest all along.

❖ ❖ ❖

Today's Recipe:

Christmas Eve Fried Oysters

Ingredients:

1 quart small oysters
2 cups panko or gluten-free breadcrumbs
4 eggs, beaten
1/2 cup butter
2 tablespoons olive oil

1/8 teaspoon salt
ground pepper to taste

Directions:

1. Crack eggs and remove eggs from shells. Drop yolks and whites into the same bowl. Beat eggs with a fork.
2. Drain the oysters in a colander and then spoon them, 4 to 5 at a time, into the beaten eggs.
3. Gently spoon the oysters from the egg mixture into your bread or cracker crumbs or panko.
4. Add more oysters to the egg mixture to create a rotation.
5. Add a third of the butter and 1 tablespoon of olive oil to a skillet and heat to medium.
6. Gently transfer the oysters that are in the crumbs to the melted butter and oil combination in the skillet. Transfer the oysters in the beaten eggs to the crumbs and refill the bowl of beaten eggs with 4 to 5 additional oysters. Continue the rotation.
7. Salt and pepper the oysters on the medium hot skillet.
8. Fry both sides of the oysters, but not too hot, as you don't want them to burn. Turn oysters carefully, so as not to disturb the crust that is forming.

Serve immediately, while warm, with lemon juice and tartar sauce. Leftovers are very good served cold the following day in an oyster burger with mayonnaise and tartar sauce.

DAY NINE

The Greatest Gift

When God the Father sent His only son Jesus Christ to Earth to be the perfect sacrifice in our place, He gave humanity the greatest gift of all time. John 15:13 states, *"Greater love hath no man than this, that a man lay down his life for his friends."*

The best gift we can give is the gift of love, and a wonderful way to demonstrate that is by offering prayer. It is impossible to genuinely pray for someone for a period of time and continue to have unkind thoughts or ill-will toward them. Jesus knew this and said in Matthew 5:44, *"But I say unto you, love your enemies, bless them that curse you, do good to them that hate you, and pray for them which despitefully use you and persecute you."*

Whew. That's a tall order. God wants us to live in harmony with Him and with each other. And in His eyes, we are all equal, all sinners, and all His children who need His grace and salvation.

God answers our prayers because of His mercy, not our good works. While as Christians we are called to follow God's word and live a life in the steps of Christ, it is not our obedience that persuades God to answer our prayers but rather His mercy and grace toward us.

The prophet Daniel understood this when he was praying on behalf of the Jews who were exiled in Babylon. *"We do not make requests of you because we are righteous, but rather because of Your great mercy."* Daniel 9:18.

Sometimes God leads us into a period of unplanned (by us) waiting in our own lives so that we can redirect our focus to praying for and helping those He places in our path. What if we changed lenses and instead of seeing this as a detour, we chose to see it through His eyes, as a time and opportunity to participate in the growth and development of those He brings into our lives?

Not everyone believes in prayer or wants to hear that you are praying for them. This is not a hall pass to write them off. And it doesn't mean that they cannot or will not benefit from prayer. But it does mean that if you want to bring down their defenses, you pray for them silently, and quietly, asking that they are protected and their needs are met. They may not respond to you or on your timetable, but prayer is always impactful. Sincere prayers are never wasted.

The difference between canning pickles and God's providence is that God's calendar is not shared. When canning sweet pickles, the recipe guarantees when the pickles will be ready. God's time is not scheduled. Repeatedly in the Bible, and even in spiritual circles, we are reminded that *No man knows the day or hour. Matthew 24*.

This passage is referring to the return of Christ, but even when the angels first alerted Elizabeth about the birth of John the Baptist or Mary about the birth of Jesus, they never issued an exact date with the prophesy. In many places the Bible points to signs or things to watch for or confirm, but never in the Bible is a prophecy followed by a specific date and hour.

I called my Aunt Dorthy to ask her about some of her favorite childhood meals her mom made. She was quick to respond: "Everything she made was delicious."

When I asked her for a favorite recipe, she had to think about it. "Well ya see, mom grew almost everything we ate. She had a huge garden in the summer and canned everything we didn't eat at the time for meals the rest of the year."

Like so many, she rarely used actual recipes. Her recipes started with the same ingredient: LOVE.

Grandma Ursula loved her family and she loved making them delicious meals.

After a bit of conversation, Aunt Dorthy did come up with a few favorites. She especially loved her mom's meatloaf and garden burgers, where Grandma Ursula sautéed beef patties along with "whatever was in her garden or basement that she had already canned."

Funny thing: those are two of my dad's favorite dishes too. Maybe it was the food, or just maybe, it was the love. While no formal recipe for either of these dishes exists today, as a little girl, Dorthy watched her mom. Since she makes her garden burger patties the same way, I just had to rephrase the question.

Aunt Dorthy, How do you make garden burgers? When I re-phrased it, she was happy to share.

Today's Recipe:

<u>Grandma Ursula's Garden Burgers</u>

<u>(as told by Aunt Dorthy)</u>

Ingredients:

2 pounds ground beef
1 large onion, finely diced
1 each red, yellow and green peppers

1 quart stewed tomatoes or 4 pounds fresh tomatoes, peeled and chopped
2 cups zucchini, peeled and chopped
1/8 teaspoon salt
ground pepper to taste

Directions:

1. Clean and chop vegetables into bite-size pieces.
2. Form 6 round hamburger patties out of 2 pounds of lean hamburger.
3. Place the 6 patties into a large skillet and then place vegetables around and on top of beef.
4. Salt and pepper meat and vegetables. Sautee on medium heat.
5. Turn meat once and continue to cook until vegetables are soft and meat is to your preferred doneness.
6. Serve with buns, bread or alone on plate.

DAY TEN

The Making of Sweet Pickles

In Luke 5, Jesus Christ is out on the Sea of Galilee with his disciples, many who were fishermen by trade. He had just completed a miraculous catch of fish and his followers were in awe. It was then than He called them to formally move away from their livelihoods as fishermen, to join Him in becoming fishers of men – sharing the good news and gospel of God's love to all people.

While we wait for God to answer the important prayers in our lives, we can invest our time in making sweet pickles in the lives of those around us.

So, what does it mean to make sweet pickles in the lives of people around us? It means to intercede on their behalf, bringing their petitions to God. It is one of the greatest gifts we can give others.

This is not an empty promise of casually praying for someone when they cross our minds. This is an intentional practice of regularly praying for someone with their permission and their cooperation. It's serving as the brine that will transform their cucumbers into sweet pickles.

A couple of years ago, an unexplained set of circumstances unfolded that brought a family I didn't know into my circle of awareness. The father, a physician I had professionally crossed paths with a decade before, had been diagnosed with Stage IV colon cancer.

One day, on the way to lap swim at a local pool, one of my swim mates, shared her sadness and emotion about an anonymous patient who she had performed scans on as part of her job. Because of HIPAA, all she could tell me was that he had young children and his situation was grave.

She asked me to pray for this anonymous man, and I did. My first prayer for him went something like this: *Father, I have no idea who this man is, but you do. You know his name and count the hairs on his head. You know his situation, his condition, his fears, his challenges both with his disease as well as what he is facing spiritually and emotionally. I lift him and his family up to You for Your perfect touch, and for Your perfect healing in this life or the next. Amen.*

A few days later, I saw a public CaringBridge notice for a local doctor, and having worked in healthcare, I shared it on my Facebook page.

It was much later that I realized the two were connected. Over the next few weeks, God continually brought this physician from the CaringBridge post and his family to my mind for prayer.

Weeks turned into months and God started prompting me to reach out and deliver messages directly to the physician, whose health was quickly declining. God had placed him and his family into my prayer life as a sweet pickle – a prayer request that would require persistent prayer and a great deal of waiting.

I would pray and wait. Pray and wait – often unsure why God chose me. It had been a very rough year in my own life and here God was pressing me to invest my prayers into this family I didn't know. So I followed His prompting.

One day, I received a message from God that He would walk the physician through his battle with cancer, and he would be com-

Sweet Pickles Take Time

pletely healed. Then I got prompted to deliver that message.

This felt like an overwhelmingly heavy burden, and I resisted delivering this news.

According to all medical evidence, he was dying. It was so clear. He was diagnosed at Stage IV, his complications were increasing and his health was declining. Anyone reading his CaringBridge updates could clearly see where this was going. *Except God had a totally didn't plan for him, and He chose me to deliver this message. This physician was about to receive a miracle and I was chosen to deliver the news.*

That sounds amazing in a movie or a book after-the-fact. But imagine this from his family's perspective, his wife's perspective. She's caring for the man she loves, on some level preparing to care for their children after his death, when a stranger sends her husband a text that says: *God's going to walk you through this. You're going to be healed.*

I worried how that would make her feel. I don't know what that was like for her, but I think it would have made me angry. Perhaps I would have used the term so many people reach for and use on people who disagree with them – ignorant.

This request stressed me. I worried: *What if I'm wrong? What will that do to his wife? What will that do to him? What would they think of me? Why is God putting this on my heart when my own life is falling apart? I have enough of my own stuff to think about.*

But it wasn't about me. This miracle was never about me. It wasn't my message. It wasn't from me and it wasn't for me. I was gifted with tickets to a front row seat to see God's beautiful and miraculous hand at work. I was the chosen vehicle to deliver this message of life-saving hope. But it came down to one question first: *Would I step outside my comfort zone and do in faith what God was asking?*

Reluctantly, and not with a joyful heart, I obeyed. I delivered the news that God would walk him through this, not merely "with him" through this journey. *God would fully heal him.* And can you guess how this physician responded?

Exactly how I feared. With silence. For a very long time.

I would regularly check my phone, impatiently waiting for his important text to come in, thanking me for sharing the good news or telling me "it miraculously happened and he was healed." More silence.

I wanted to rush his outcome. I wanted to hear that he was healthy and cancer-free. I wanted to hear that he was happy to receive the message I had passed along. But all I got was radio silence.

I couldn't blame him. He was undergoing many surgeries and chemotherapy treatments. Radiation. It was grim, for a while. But by this time, he was my sweet pickle. Before this, he had agreed that he wanted and appreciated my prayers, and he continued to update me on his progress. The challenge had been accepted and all I could do was faithfully pray for him and his family. And wait. I had committed to wait this out and watch God's miracle unfold. I prayed for him and his family, without any response for a long time.

Finally the physician responded to my text. Once again, he expressed that he was thankful for my message and prayers. And once again, he updated me on his journey – which at this point included some improvement but by no means full healing.

A few months later, I stopped praying, and my communication with the physician ended.

The physician was miraculously healed. After a series of surgeries and treatments, he was determined to be in full remission, no longer receiving treatment. God had walked him through his cancer, and he was healthy again, just as promised.

What a magnificent display of God's healing power this turned out to be. There, in the middle of my greatest struggle, when my own faith was shaken over events and loss in my life, God gave me a front row seat to experience a genuine miracle.

I never became friends with the physician or his family. I don't keep up with them. God brought them into my life for a season, for their betterment and for mine. In *Romans 8:28* we are reminded that as Christians, we are called according to God's purpose. God used my willingness to deliver key scripture verses and messages to a man I didn't know. And God delivered on every promise. *Deliverance didn't come on my timing or in the way I expected. But He delivered exactly as He said He would.*

As a child, one salad stands out as sister's and my most requested dish for birthdays, Easter, Christmas Eve and other special occasions. This was no doubt one of those recipes passed down through the ages. Mom called it "7-Layer Salad." Grandma Ida Mae made it, as did Grandma Eva. No doubt, mothers and grandmothers with gardens from many generations back have made the 7-Layer salad for family reunions, church picnics and gatherings of all types big and small. The best part is you can easily customize the inside ingredients. If you don't like green onions, radishes make an excellent swap.

Today's Recipe:

Grandma's 7-Layer Salad

Ingredients:

6 cups iceberg lettuce, torn
2 cups celery, crosscut
1/2 cup green onions, thinly sliced
1 can black olives
1 cup frozen petite peas
1 cup mayonnaise

Debra Yergen

2 cups cheddar cheese, grated

Directions:

1. Layer a large glass bowl with the following ingredients starting with lettuce, celery, green onions, olives, and frozen petite peas.
2. Smooth on a layer of mayonnaise, topped with grated cheddar cheese.
3. Stir just before serving. The peas may be slightly frozen but will thaw quickly when tossed with the other ingredients. This will keep your salad crisp and safe.

NOTE: It's important to have the frozen peas just below the mayonnaise to keep it cold, especially if traveling to a picnic or outing with this beautiful salad that looks stunning on any table.

DAY ELEVEN

Let's Get Cooking

Most of my friends know about the sweet pickles I create in a jar. But the more important sweet pickles, the life-changing sweet pickles, are the people I pray for daily.

Prayer wasn't always such a priority to me. For most of my life, prayer was something I participated in almost like an "extra activity" for good measure. Growing up, I didn't really understand the significance of prayer as a foundational necessity in my life. I learned the true value of prayer from a set of surrogate grandparents from our church, who lovingly adopted our family when my sister and I were little. They always talked about praying for us.

Sadly, I finally and fully understood the significance of their prayers when they passed away in 2010. I physically, mentally and spiritually felt the loss of their prayers in my life after they left this earth. My life was never as consistently difficult while they were living as it has been since they have passed.

While I know my parents, sister, and friends do pray for me now at various times (they tell me and I can often sense the protection that comes with their prayers, especially through specific battles), I miss the consistent prayers for protection that I felt while my surrogate grandparents were alive. It was an invisible shield that nothing since then has replaced.

I was Grandpa Short's sweet pickle. He prayed for me day-after-day, week-after-week and year-after-year. He was not a man of great earthly achievements, but he was a man of great faith and spiritual power. When I feel called to pray for someone and commit to them as my sweet pickle, I can only aim to live with the same integrity and faith Grandpa Short demonstrated by his example.

The truth is, *Sweet Pickles Take Time.* They take time in the canning process and sometimes they take time in prayer.

There's a man who has been one of my sweet pickles for nearly a year. I was certain he would be healed by now, but that is not my call. I am only called to pray and stay in faith that God is working. And as long as God continues to place him on my heart, I will continue to pray and trust that God has a plan. I am not even sure that he knows I pray for him, but his wife knows, and she updates me on his pain and progress.

God knows that we humans are naturally impatient. We have been impatient throughout time. In Psalm 5:3, King David writes, *"In the morning, O Lord, you hear my voice; in the morning I lay my requests before you and wait in expectation."*

Just like waiting on edible pickles, the recipe for sweet pickles in prayer also requires time. In fact, each batch takes 13 weeks. Thirteen weeks is three months or one entire season.

This is a great undertaking in praying for someone faithfully. At the end of the 13 weeks, God may bring new people into your life or you may be asked to spend another season praying for the same person. Only you will know. Either way, the outcome will be delicious, because as you lift up others in prayer, you will also be lifted up and nourished along the path.

Today's Recipe:

Spiritual Sweet Pickles

Ingredients:

A humble heart
A desire to serve
Faithfulness to keep praying
Acceptance of the outcome

Directions:

1. **Pray for God to bring someone into your life or mind.** You might see a post on social media. Or you may uncover a lost or misplaced item. You may run into someone at the grocery store or something else entirely may happen that you hadn't planned. It may be someone close to you or someone you don't know. There's no need to try to find it. It will find you. Just pray and wait. It's that simple.

2. **Make a connection.** Prayer is powerful and if you are going to be praying over someone, you need to make sure that they are not only open to this but that they (or someone close to them) are partnering with you in your journey to make spiritual sweet pickles.

The exchange can go something like this:

    YOU: God has placed you on my heart. I'd like to pray for you for the next 13 weeks. Will you participate with me in this?

    THEM: What do I need to do?

    YOU: I need for you to share with me something I can pray about. Then I need for you to write down times you experience a feeling, sign or activity related to your prayer request.

    THEM: I can do that.

    YOU: I need one more thing. I need you to update me on any progress or miracles you see. If the progress is too personal, let me know that you're seeing progress.

NOTE: Why an update? Why can't we pray for someone without their participation? Well, we can, but a partnership requires a commitment on both sides. We can pray for anyone (any cucumber) at any time. Sweet pickles are a bigger investment.

When I ask my friends or family for prayer and they surround me like a heavenly army of angels, I feel the impact of their prayers in the moment. But when the battle ends, they move on, because I am their cucumber, not their sweet pickle.

The sweet pickle relationship goes both ways. It's a partnership. I regularly updated my grandparents what was going on in my life. They knew what to pray for and they reminded me often that they loved me and prayed for me. I only wish now that I would have appreciated this gift more while I had them.

Committing to a pickle is faith-building for the pickle and you. They will be inspired to watch for God's hand at work. And the faith-affirming process will reconfirm to you that your prayers are heard and answered.

Walking in faith means different things to different people, and sometimes different things at different times in our lives. This is something you will just know, and not something you ever have to force.

Not everyone you pray for is going to be a sweet pickle, or maybe not a sweet pickle at a specific time. We all have freewill. God calls but it's our choice to respond. Usually, when God has brought someone to your heart for prayer, they need help and welcome the intervention of prayer. But if not, simply pray them back in God's hands without evaluation or judgment. *Matthew 7:5* reminds us: *First take the log out of your own eye, and then you will see clearly to take the speck out of your brother's eye.*

It's such a treat to hear someone talk about a person they loved. I only met Grandma Ida Mae as an infant, but her legacy lives on through those who loved her. Sometimes when I am cooking or

Sweet Pickles Take Time

doing dishes, I feel a warmth around me, and I'm sure it's Ida Mae (or Susie) looking after me. I was her first grandbaby and the only grandchild she ever met.

When I called Isabelle to learn about some of grandma's recipes, she mostly pointed out favorites from soup cans, mayonnaise jars, cornstarch containers and of course her trusted red and white Betty Crocker cookbook.

Then all at once, her voice grew light when she shared a recipe she made every year for Susie (yes, that's what Isabelle called Grandma Ida Mae) on her birthday. I asked her the name and she said, "I don't know that it had a name. It was a delightful raspberry surprise." So that's what I named it here.

Today's Recipe:

Izzy's Delightful Raspberry Surprise

Ingredients:

3 boxes of raspberry Jell-O™
1 angel food cake, a few days or a few weeks old
2 cups fresh raspberries, divided
2 cups whipped cream

Directions:

1. Prepare the Jell-O, according to the box. Pour it into a Tupperware container or a round kitchen bowl.
2. Tear up pieces of an angel food cake and poke them down into the Jell-O just as it starts to set up. Fill the Jell-O as full as you can get it.
3. Put a plate on top and refrigerate.
4. Whip up 2 cups of cream with a mixer to get it really fluffy.
5. Fold in two thirds of your berries

6. When the Jell-O is firm, turn it upside down on the plate and frost the Jell-O dome with the berry whipped cream. Pour the remaining berries on top.

According to Isabelle (Izzy as we call her) this recipe "Looks impressive and it's real simple." Because this recipe was given to me from her memory, I had a few more questions.

ME: Did you use raspberry extract for flavor?

IZZY: Oh honey, I didn't have extract. We had a cow and a raspberry bush. I churned my own butter and cream and picked the raspberries in the backyard.

ME: Did you have real Jell-O back then or did you make your own with pectin?

IZZY: It came in a little box like today, only it was real cheap. We made salads, desserts and everything out of that.

ME: Where did you get the angel food cake?

IZZY: Well that was a process. I made it from scratch, separated my own eggs and baked it in a wood stove. Not electric like you have today. It didn't always turn out. But even if it fell, it didn't matter. I tore it into pieces and it was perfect in Jell-O.

Every time I hang up the phone after a conversation with Izzy, my mouth hurts from smiling and laughing so hard. I can only hope I bring my friends and family as much joy as Cousin Isabelle brings to all of us.

DAY TWELVE

Teach Us To Pray

Jesus Christ taught us how to pray using two variations of The Lord's Prayer, which appear in both Luke 11 and the more familiar *Matthew 6:9-13: Our Father who art in heaven, hallowed be thy name. Thy kingdom come. Thy will be done, on earth as it is in heaven. Give us this day our daily bread; and forgive us our trespasses, as we forgive those who trespass against us; and lead us not into temptation but deliver us from evil. For Thine is the kingdom and the power and the glory forever and ever. Amen.*

I used to wonder why people said "Amen" all the time. Amen is the same word used in Hebrew, Greek and Latin. It means truth or "It is so." It would be the Biblical equivalent of people today simply agreeing with what was said, or more casually saying, "Totally, dude."

For all the various denominations and interpretations of Christians around the world, *The Lord's Prayer* provides a sense of cohesion and solidarity to unite believers.

Much has been said about breaking this prayer into parts. Some theologians point out that the first three of the petitions in Matthew address God and the next four are related to human needs and concerns.

The overall message of *The Lord's Prayer* is our understanding that we the creation lean into our Creator for our needs, hopes, desires and of course forgiveness. Just as God forgives us, loves us and delivers us, we respond by extending His grace to other people. He is more than our Savior; we were created in His image and therefore He is our example of how to live.

As we express gratitude for what God has done, our blessings expand. God is gracious and generous, although, with our limited human view, we cannot see the whole picture. We want something beautiful on the outside that God knows contains a worm or poison within, and in His grace sometimes He removes what we think is beautiful from our lives

When this happens it can sometimes feel crippling to understand but in *James 1:17* He tells us, *"Every good and perfect gift is from above, coming down from the Father."* Is this not worth our thanksgiving, even when circumstances do not work out as we hoped?

Many people keep a gratitude jar with a paper and pen close by so that each time they experience a blessing big or small, they watch the folded pieces of paper stack up in the jar. In the same way, some people keep a jar or journal of answered prayers and observed blessings.

Albert Einstein is famously quoted as saying, "The more I learn, the more I realize how much I don't know." Everything about God is infinitely greater than anything the human mind can imagine. And yet, He seeks to have a personal relationship with each and every person who lives. Isn't that truly incredible?

The God of the Universe loves, cares about, wants to know us, and wants to hear from each and every one of us?

I saved my favorite recipe for last. It's something my mom made when sister and I were growing up to celebrate both happy occasions and to comfort us when life knocked us over.

To me, mom's Swedish meatballs were comfort food of the highest order. There are a handful of friends who've been invited for

Sweet Pickles Take Time

dinner with mom's Swedish meatballs. It's a sign someone is very special.

I'm not sure what makes them Swedish, by the way. Most Swedish meatballs have a gravy or cream sauce, not a tomato base like this one. But these are mom's and these are my absolute favorite. I hope they enhance a special occasion for you too, or bring just the right amount of comfort on a day you need something tangy and warm.

NOTE: Back in the day when this recipe was first passed down, most folks were poor, and they made everything stretch as far as it could. Today, more people can afford to add a little extra vinegar, sugar and Worcestershire sauce. It's really the sauce that makes this dish so special. You could easily make this dish by substituting ground turkey or maybe even ground mushrooms and vegetables for the beef. Although, it's hard to beat mom's version.

Today's Recipe:

Mom's Amazing Swedish Meatballs

Ingredients for meatballs:

1 pound ground beef (mom uses a ground beef-pork mixture)
1/2 cup rolled uncooked oats (mom prefers instant oats as she feels they have a finer texture)
2/3 cup cream or evaporated milk
2 tablespoons - finely chopped onion
1/8 teaspoon pepper
1/2 teaspoon salt

Ingredients for sauce:

Over the years, family cooks have used a range of ingredient measurements. I've included the range below, so you can adapt this to you individual taste. Mom's recommendations are in parenthesis.

1 1/2 -2 tablespoons of Worcestershire sauce (mom uses 2T)
1 1/2 - 2 tablespoons vinegar (mom uses 2T)
1 1/2 - 2 tablespoons of sugar (mom uses 2T)
1/2 -2/3 cup ketchup (mom uses half a cup)
1/3-1/2 cup water (mom uses 1/3 cup)
4 tablespoons minced onion

Directions:

1. Heat oven to 350 degrees.
2. Mix together the whipping cream and the instant oats and let sit for 10 minutes.
3. Finely chop the onion, dividing it into a portion for the meatballs and a portion for the sauce.
4. Mix together all the sauce ingredients to give the flavors a chance to blend. This is the original recipe's "sauce" volume for one pound of meat, but that's not how mom makes it. Since our family loves the sauce (and who doesn't love sauce?) mom makes one and a half times as much sauce for 1 pound and 3 times as much sauce for 2 pounds of meat.
5. Returning to the meatballs, fold the oatmeal mixture into the hamburger and add salt and pepper.
6. Form meatballs and place in a 9x13 pan.
7. Pour the sauce over the meatballs.
8. Bake for 1 hour.

Mom describes this as a "forgiving recipe." The flavor is amazing but hearing it's forgiving makes it even more special. Mom says this is an easy recipe to add to when more people are coming to dinner. She says you can prepare it and freeze it raw to cook later, or cook it and freeze leftovers.

Thank you for taking this 12-day journey with me. I hope your heart and stomach are nourished and filled with joy.

Thank you for exploring with me why *Sweet Pickles Take Time*, and the gifts that come when we trust God's plan, even when it doesn't make sense. Life can be very hard. And some people seem to get a bigger helping of challenges than others. But there is always respite in God's love and grandmas' recipes. These two things have carried me so far, and I hope they bring comfort to you too.

The End.

Made in the USA
Monee, IL
03 September 2024